THE KREUTZER SONATA

Borgo Press Books by FERNAND NOZIÈRE

The Kreutzer Sonata: A Play in Four Acts (with Alfred Savoir)

Other Plays Adapted from the Works of LEO TOLSTOY

Anna Karenina, by Edmond Guiraud
War and Peace, by J. Wladimir Bienstock & Charles Martel

THE KREUTZER SONATA

A PLAY IN FOUR ACTS

FERNAND NOZIÈRE &

ALFRED SAVOIR

Adapted from the Novel by Leo Tolstoy

Translated by Frank J. Morlock

THE BORGO PRESS
MMXII

THE KREUTZER SONATA

Copyright © 2002, 2012 by Frank J. Morlock

FIRST BORGO PRESS EDITION

Published by Wildside Press LLC

www.wildsidebooks.com

DEDICATION

For my dear friend, Marthe Rodríguez

CONTENTS

CAST OF CHARACTERS. 9
ACT ONE 11
ACT TWO 59
ACT THREE 119
ACT FOUR. 173
ABOUT THE AUTHOR 207

CAST OF CHARACTERS

Poznichev

Troukhasinsky

Uncle

Doctor Ivanoff

Gregor

Laura

Mother

Vera

Chambermaid

ACT ONE

A large stage, somewhat in disorder as if after a move. In a corner a trunk. An impression of luxury.

Poznichev is seated before a table his head wrapped in a towel. A chambermaid crosses the room. Poznichev stops her with a gesture.

POZNICHEV

And Madame?

CHAMBERMAID

Not yet ready—

POZNICHEV

My God, I'm bored (She starts to leave) You will tell her that I am bored: have her come.

CHAMBERMAID

Fine, Sir.

POZNICHEV

If Madame asks you what I am doing, you will tell her I'm not doing a thing because I am bored.

CHAMBERMAID

Fine, Sir.

POZNICHEV

It's odd—when Madame is here I am less bored.

CHAMBERMAID

Madame will soon have completed dressing—If the gentleman would like to go—

POZNICHEV

No I don't wish to—I'm tired—(The maid leaves. Uncle enters)

POZNICHEV

(Rising) Hello, Uncle.

UNCLE

How are you? And your wife?

POZNICHEV

(Infatuated) Oh—very well. You are sweet to come see us this way—unexpectedly.

UNCLE

I learned that you'd returned.

POZNICHEV

Yesterday evening by the ten o'clock train.

UNCLE

(Smiling) The honeymoon trip.

POZNICHEV

(Smiling) The honeymoon.

UNCLE

And what follows—the headache.

POZNICHEV

(Laughing) No—why do you think I have a headache?

UNCLE

Hell—(Pointing to the towel)

POZNICHEV

Ah—that. (Pulling it off with irritation)

UNCLE

You are annoyed?

POZNICHEV

(Angrily) My wife would have been able to see me like this. It's grotesque!

UNCLE

(Kindly) No indeed, no indeed.

POZNICHEV

What would she have thought of me?

UNCLE

That you are subject to migraines in the morning.

POZNICHEV

What's this—or rather what are the inconveniences of the quarantine!

UNCLE

(Taking Poznichev's arm) Come to me. You can tell

me. I'm a doctor. Are you this way often?

POZNICHEV

I never have headaches.

UNCLE

Your eyes seem tired.

POZNICHEV

That proves nothing.

UNCLE

Perhaps. You're not sick?

POZNICHEV

(Annoyed) No, uncle.

UNCLE

For sure?

POZNICHEV

I am telling you.

UNCLE

During the honeymoon trip you were careful?

POZNICHEV

(Furious) No—I wasn't careful! Why should I be careful? I'm very well, marvelous! I've never been better. That's all! (He is furious) Let's speak of something else if you will? (A pause)

UNCLE

You were happy with your trip?

POZNICHEV

Ravished.

UNCLE

You went to Italy.

POZNICHEV

As far as Naples.

UNCLE

Ah—Italy!

POZNICHEV

Yes! A few too many monuments, perhaps.

UNCLE

(Conciliatory) Perhaps.

POZNICHEV

But apart from that, it's beautiful; especially in the countryside, it's very beautiful. Those mountains—at first when you get to the summit—the snow— scintillating. Only, as it was storming—we didn't see the snow. And it was the same way at Florence. At Florence we lost our trunks, then it was the mountains again; to the right and the left there were these poor lime trees, nothing at all. At Rome we lost our baggage again—At Naples it was Vesuvius. Ah! Vesuvius.

UNCLE

It was beautiful?

POZNICHEV

(With conviction) Very beautiful, indeed; indeed, that really hit me.

UNCLE

Really?

POZNICHEV

You must have seen such things—that gives you a—

religious feeling.

UNCLE

You are exaggerating!

POZNICHEV

No use being a strong-minded person—there are certain spectacles of nature that a man cannot resist. I would never have thought that a volcanic eruption would raise such sentiments in me (He rises, walks about and sighs admiringly) Ah! Vesuvius! A marvel! You know, uncle, I would like to go to America.

UNCLE

To do what?

POZNICHEV

To see Niagara (He is pensive. A pause)

UNCLE

And naturally you are happy with your wife?

POZNICHEV

(Bored) Naturally!

UNCLE

I ask you this because I advised you against marrying.

POZNICHEV

Yes, you have ideas of a confirmed bachelor.

UNCLE

No—Only I think that you must marry very young—or never marry!

POZNICHEV

That's only a theory. I've lived—but like all men of a certain class, later I settled down, married like everyone else—I am not an exception; thus, I regret nothing.

UNCLE

Bravo!

POZNICHEV

(A silence, then abruptly) Why do you want me to be unhappy? My father, my uncle, my friends were perfectly happy in their honeymoon. As for me, I did like them, I married a pure, candid, pretty young girl—a virgin—like them, I went to Italy—Heavens, at Florence, we stopped in the—where my parents spent their first night. Perhaps we had the same room. That's touching, isn't it? Italy? Italy? Why wouldn't I be happy? I'm not looking from noon to four.

UNCLE

So much the better. Your wife loves you?

POZNICHEV

Yes she loves me! Yes, she loves me! She's joyous, Laura, in her happiness, as with a new toy. She's a little girl even!—Even—(Stopping)

UNCLE

What?

POZNICHEV

No.

UNCLE

Look—

POZNICHEV

Well, at bottom, Laura loves me more than I love her. Ah—that's astonishing!

UNCLE

Rather.

POZNICHEV

Still, that's the way it is (He whistles) You don't think so?

UNCLE

With women, everything is possible.

POZNICHEV

But what's happened to me then is perfectly logical. I'm only thirty-five—without having abused my youth, I wasted it.

UNCLE

Mostly.

POZNICHEV

I'm only a little blasé—It had pleasures which left me indifferent. I'm no longer a collegian who screwed things up. But she—

UNCLE

She is young.

POZNICHEV

Madly! And to think that if I weren't here, she with her nature, with her temperament would have married a very rich fellow.

UNCLE

Is it true that her parents have debts?

POZNICHEV

What a deception I spared her from! The poor little thing! She might have met a rake, of which there are so many. Was that child lucky to have met me! How lucky she was!

UNCLE

And you?

POZNICHEV

As for me I am happy to be able to protect her.

UNCLE

That's all. That suffices for you?

POZNICHEV

You know me uncle—I don't have one of those frivolous natures content with the present time. I reflected: I've never been happy. But this time, the sensation—very plain of giving happiness has softened, moved me—when I see her smile, gratefully, I pull her to me to kiss her—what I would like to reach in her is not her lips but her smile. That's a delicious sensation.

UNCLE

A bit tiresome.

POZNICHEV

No, no, it's a delicious feeling.

UNCLE

Then she's happy.

POZNICHEV

(Anxious) Absolutely. She wouldn't play games, would she?

UNCLE

There's no reason—

POZNICHEV

A young girl raised in the country.

UNCLE

(Looking at his watch) It's getting late.

POZNICHEV

No, no—I won't let you leave. You are going to say hello to my wife. You will let me know your impression. (Stupidly) You'll see. (Rings, the maid comes in) You will beg Madame to come right away. Right away.

CHAMBERMAID

Right, sir. (She leaves)

POZNICHEV

(Embarrassed) Excuse me, uncle. Are you planning to kiss Laura when she gets here?

UNCLE

Why I don't know.

POZNICHEV

It's the custom—I know yet it's not a reasonable custom, is it?

UNCLE

I am unfortunately at the age when kisses leave me

cold.

POZNICHEV

Right. Exactly then. There's no use for you to kiss her! (Shaking his hand effusively) You aren't angry with me?

UNCLE

You please me greatly.

LAURA

(Entering) Hello, Uncle. (Shaking his hand) Did I make you wait?

UNCLE

No, indeed.

LAURA

I needed some time to dress. The trunks were not unpacked!

POZNICHEV

(Radiant) And then she got up late, very late.

LAURA

Yes, I had a lazy morning!

POZNICHEV

Like every day.

UNCLE

It's a bad habit.

POZNICHEV

Don't scold her Uncle. She adores it, don't you, Laura?

LAURA

(Indecisive) Certainly, my friend.

POZNICHEV

Every morning, I'm the one who has to remind her that it's time for me to get up! Right?

LAURA

It's true.

UNCLE

Even at your mother's?

LAURA

(Smiling quickly) In the country, one rises early—at six o'clock, sometimes sooner. At dawn I was breathing the air of the forest.

POZNICHEV

Little dreamer! But you were alone—now there are two to dream.

LAURA

Yes.

POZNICHEV

Look at her, Uncle—Don't you find her changed?

UNCLE

(To Laura) You've gotten a bit pale.

LAURA

Really?

POZNICHEV

It goes well with her, doesn't it? She's no longer the young girl of yesterday; she's a woman—a woman!

UNCLE

You are charming but you must get your fine complexion back.

POZNICHEV

Huh?

LAURA

I am very well, I assure you. (Laura coughs)

POZNICHEV

(Turning abruptly and going to Laura) You coughed?

LAURA

You are mistaken.

POZNICHEV

Yes—you coughed.

LAURA

(repressing the cough) Perhaps!

POZNICHEV

You've got influenza—

LAURA

It's nothing.

POZNICHEV

(Uneasy) Heavens, you've lost your voice (To Uncle) Hasn't she —?

UNCLE

Why—

POZNICHEV

I beg you (Laura coughs) You caught a cold last night. I told you so—You have no idea how delicate she is. She is overworked. (To Laura) You are going to go to bed.

LAURA

But I am not sick!

UNCLE

It's not necessary.

POZNICHEV

Not necessary? You are going to go to bed—don't argue, my child. And who will stay with the little thing all day?—I will! I will read her pretty stories. You are going to be satisfied. Tell it to Uncle, that will please him.

LAURA

(reconciled) Certainly.

POZNICHEV

You say this in a way.

LAURA

I know you. You are going to keep me in bed for three days and as for me, I feel the need to move about, to budge. I can't live this way. If I listened to you I'd spend my whole life in bed. (Poznichev laughs) Why are you laughing? Don't laugh.

POZNICHEV

(Going to her) Child. (To Uncle) You'd say she was fifteen at least.

UNCLE

She's delicious. As for me, my friends, I am going to leave you. I am late for my visits.

LAURA

Wait a minute. Paul will accompany you.

POZNICHEV

(Smiling) Is this the way you get rid of me?

LAURA

Exactly.

POZNICHEV

And you—you will stay alone?

LAURA

I will read.

POZNICHEV

What novel?

LAURA

I don't know.

POZNICHEV

I don't want you to bore yourself.

LAURA

It will do your lungs good.

POZNICHEV

(Nettled) Hold on a minute. If my presence displeases you, say so?

LAURA

(Embarrassed) No—how can you think?

POZNICHEV

In that case —?

LAURA

(Quickly) You'll walk, you'll pass by a nice shop—you will buy me something, that's all.

POZNICHEV

Ah, ah, ah—little Laura!

LAURA

Yes, yes, I am a child!

POZNICHEV

(Reassured) I don't bore you.

UNCLE

No indeed, no indeed.

POZNICHEV

I am going to find my hat. I am with you in a minute. (He leaves)

UNCLE

(Looking fixedly at Laura) Absorbing my nephew?— Eh?

LAURA

(Embarrassed) He's a fine lad.

UNCLE

Indeed I think so!

LAURA

(A pause) Tell me, Uncle: Natrimoff's one of your friends?

UNCLE

I was very close to his father.

LAURA

You know it's a question of marriage between him and my sister?

UNCLE

Indeed.

LAURA

Does he still cling to that marriage?

UNCLE

Why do you ask me that? Is he displeasing your sister?

LAURA

I don't think so.

UNCLE

In that case?

LAURA

My sister is quite young to get married.

UNCLE

No indeed.

LAURA

Why yes, she's only seventeen.

UNCLE

And you?

LAURA

I'm eighteen.

UNCLE

Natrimoff is a fine lad, he will do her good.

LAURA

What do you know about it? Now she is happy, she does what she wants, she sleeps peacefully.

UNCLE

We'll talk about it again. This is not the moment. I must leave and this morning you appear to me to be a bit exhausted, a little irritable, too.

LAURA

My head weighs on me, it is heavy.

UNCLE

It's the trip which must have exhausted you.

LAURA

Each morning it's the same feeling. But don't say anything to Poznichev.

UNCLE

Why's that?

LAURA

He'll stay.

POZNICHEV

(Entering, to Uncle) Are you coming?

UNCLE

(Rising, to Laura) Bye.

POZNICHEV

Where are we going?

UNCLE

On the quai.

POZNICHEV

Soon, Laura. I will be back in an hour at the latest.

LAURA

Yes, come back.

POZNICHEV

You won't get impatient? (They kiss for a long while) When I'm out, you'll go to the window—you'll give me a signal with your kerchief—will you?

LAURA

Certainly.

POZNICHEV

In the street, amongst strangers, I would love to see, as I turn back, the gesture of a little woman who is thinking of me. (To Uncle) Let's go. (They leave—Laura goes to the window and waves her handkerchief)

LAURA

(Waving the handkerchief) What heat—I'm choking. (A long pause) (The Chambermaid enters)

CHAMBERMAID

Madame, your mother has just arrived.

LAURA

(Joyfully) Mama!

(Laura throws herself in her mother's arms—The Chambermaid leaves)

Mama, I thought you would be here yesterday at the station, I experienced a huge disappointment in not seeing you. As I got off the train I felt myself abandoned, I wanted to weep. Vera's not accompanying you?

MOTHER

A trip in this heat would have exhausted her.

LAURA

Oh! I wanted to see her so much.

MOTHER

My big girl!

LAURA

Come, sit beside me. Speak, Mama, take me in your arms and undo my hair as you used to. (The Mother does it) Ah, it's nice, your hands in my hair. They are not hurried, they are slow, they don't tear, they don't pull—they are not doing ill!

MOTHER

What's wrong with you, my child?

LAURA

Nothing, nothing.

MOTHER

You are not sick, you are not bored?

LAURA

Not at all.

MOTHER

No clouds here?

LAURA

Oh—no.

MOTHER

In that case?

LAURA

I am exhausted, very exhausted.

MOTHER

Don't complain about it. That's the fate of newlyweds. Thanks to heaven, the marriage at least is in its infancy—it's nothing but a union of two souls.

LAURA

(Excitedly) I know, Mama, each phrase of my husband reminds me of it—for two months I've heard nothing else—day and night. In each word he places a double meaning. (Mimicking her husband's voice) You coughed. That's fine. Let's go into the room. You've caught a cold my poor child—Vesuvius has impressed you perfectly—where is the room?

MOTHER

Very fine!

LAURA

Apropos of anything and nothing, I see on his face an equivocal smile sufficiently conquering—He is satisfied.

MOTHER

I wouldn't have thought him so young.

LAURA

Enough! I've had enough of it.

MOTHER

You will regret this good time.

LAURA

It can't go on this way!

MOTHER

(Shrugging her shoulders) Are you thinking of leaving your husband because he loves you too much?

LAURA

I have no intention of leaving him. I have lots of affection for him. But I'd like to spend a week in the country, at our home, Mama, alone, like a young girl—sitting peacefully in the park on the water's shore.

MOTHER

I'd really like to take you to the country only don't you think that Poznichev would insist on accompanying you?

LAURA

(Perplexed) That's it!

MOTHER

As for me I like precise situations and I don't want to be a mother-in-law who separates her daughter from her son-in-law. Lay out the situation frankly.

LAURA

What am I going to tell him?

MOTHER

Tell him: No; he's intelligent, he will understand.

LAURA

I'm afraid of hurting him. He is so good for me! If he's obsessed with me it's from excess of affection. I am not angry with him for that.

MOTHER

If you cling to these considerations.

LAURA

All contradiction enrage him.

MOTHER

Fine business! You haven't yet heard him shout?

LAURA

Never—I wouldn't want to irritate him—he is so susceptible—to be rancorous, perhaps. I have the impression that he forgets nothing and will remember a wounding word if the occasion arises. (Poznichev's voice is heard)

POZNICHEV'S VOICE

Laura! Laura!

MOTHER

That's him?

POZNICHEV'S VOICE

Where have you hidden yourself this time, kid?

LAURA

(Nervous) You hear him? I can never hide myself—never (An uproar is heard) You hear—He's rapping the windows with his cane—now he's jostling the armchair; he's looking under the sofa. I've never hidden myself—What does this seem like?

POZNICHEV

(cocking his hat on his ear, a flower tucked in his buttonhole, offering a box with his hand to Laura. Smiling) I thought you were hiding.

LAURA

(sulkily) Really?

POZNICHEV

Ah, there you are, Mama. (Pointing with a gesture to Laura) Well—what do you think of her?

MOTHER

Changed

POZNICHEV

Embellished, isn't she? You've come for some time I hope?

MOTHER

Twelve days perhaps.

POZNICHEV

Wonderful—wonderful—It was hot in the train?

MOTHER

Suffocating and then dusty. Now I've had the delight of seeing you, my children, I'm going to change my dress.

LAURA

I'll escort you to your room.

POZNICHEV

Oh, stay with me a little—I haven't seen you for so long! (He rings, the Chambermaid enters) Show Madame her room. (To Mother) It's a bit messy, you will excuse us!

MOTHER

Yes, indeed, yes indeed—Till later! (She exits with the Chambermaid)

POZNICHEV

You didn't think I'd be back so fast?

LAURA

No.

POZNICHEV

(Happy) You see, I met some friends who wanted to detain me, but I didn't listen to them.

LAURA

(Evasively) You were wrong.

POZNICHEV

(Still happy) Why's that?

LAURA

(A pause) It would have been a distraction for you.

POZNICHEV

Can I be happy far from you? Can we be happy without each other?

LAURA

No.

POZNICHEV

(His voice a bit changed) Your Mother was there, even. You're happy that I returned rather soon?

LAURA

You didn't need to hurry.

POZNICHEV

Ah, I took a cab to get back sooner—I see I should have returned on foot (A pause)

LAURA

Don't you sometimes need solitude? Solitude is liberty. All men need a bit of liberty.

POZNICHEV

Really!

LAURA

You can't spend all your life by my skirts.

POZNICHEV

That wouldn't be so bad.

LAURA

I beg you, spare me these inanities.

POZNICHEV

(Pale) You say?

LAURA

Look: here it is three months we've been married, and I haven't had an hour for myself—myself alone.

POZNICHEV

To do what?

LAURA

You, too, I'm sure of it, you need to have recreation.

POZNICHEV

Not at all.

LAURA

Well, as for me, I need some. Like air, like water when you are thirsty. (More calmly) Often, in the middle of the night when you slept, I forced myself to remain awake—to be alone—to think all alone. I sometimes tried to slide out of bed; but without opening your eyes, you moved and I felt the weight of your hand on me.

POZNICHEV

(Letting the package fall) And as for me, who brought you a trinket...(a pause)...doubtless broken.

LAURA

I regret it.

POZNICHEV

You cause me so much pain by speaking to me this way.

LAURA

Poznichev!

POZNICHEV

I see—I've been clumsy, I've forgotten the language that must be used with children; confess that I've done the impossible to be agreeable to you?

LAURA

Yes, yes, I thank you for it.

POZNICHEV

So—smoking inconveniences you—I gave up cigarettes. It was a heavy sacrifice, still, I resigned myself to it.

LAURA

But, Poznichev, I love the odor of tobacco—but you

didn't want to listen to me.

POZNICHEV

In that case— (He goes to the table and takes a cigarette and lights it) No matter. The attention was delicate. And my favorite dog that I sent to the country because you thought he was too big.

LAURA

He was too big.

POZNICHEV

A woman's idea.

LAURA

He frightened me.

POZNICHEV

(Softened) Him? The poor animal! That was an idea. I don't reproach you in any way but I had great sorrow in separating from him—I get easily attached, it's my character—because to please you I am ready to sacrifice everything.

LAURA

I know it.

POZNICHEV

(Seated behind the table) For you, I would do anything! Heavens, the inanities that you reproach me for—do you think I care about them?

LAURA

(Violently) Then why do you do them?

POZNICHEV

(Rising) When leaving the theatre and wrapping you in your coat, I don't fail to say, "Laura, pay attention! Don't catch a cold." Do you think I truly fear for your health? Thank God, you're robust; you're in better health than I am! But isn't it touching for a serious man to linger in such childishness. I spoil you, as did your family.

LAURA

You ought to try to understand me.

POZNICHEV

Yes, indeed, I don't understand you.

LAURA

Remember, during these three months have you seen me do anything but smile, have you heard a single complaint, one cry of revolt—And yet—

POZNICHEV

(Rising, pale) And yet, what? Speak!

LAURA

(Stepping behind the sofa) No, no—It's better for me to shut up. Believe me, Poznichev, that's better for the two of us. Let's not speak of it anymore—we will forget these three months—efface them from our life.

POZNICHEV

(Violently) Why? (A pause) My God—is our discord greater than I first supposed? Speak (His voice trembling) Then—during these three months you've never been happy?

LAURA

Yes—You've given me moments of joy—of respite—if not I would have fled. An embrace sometimes makes me forget all other things. Oh—the suffering of the caresses to which we submit, the body indifferent, thought absent—You must understand—wait.

POZNICHEV

I understand. You don't love me?

LAURA

(Tenderly) Yes, indeed I love you. My words have doubtless outstripped my thoughts.

POZNICHEV

On the contrary.

LAURA

Whatever the case may be, I will keep the engagements I made in marrying you—you hear?

POZNICHEV

(Better) And you are resigning yourself—you don't refuse my ardor! In Florence where we lost our trunks—after I argued with the station master, with the porters, with the hotel porters, you thought me empty of desires! Ah, my poor little one! And in Naples where the weather was hot and torrid (A pause) After all it's natural. I've lived, I've learned to lie. But you!

LAURA

I obeyed, as all young girls—the counsel of custom (A pause)

POZNICHEV

And to say that both of us made a love-match! Because

you loved me, didn't you?

LAURA

And you? Assuredly (A pause) There's a misunderstanding between us. But now it's dissipated—in short we want the same thing. So, we shall end up creating an agreeable life for ourselves—calm, composed of sweet intimacy.

POZNICHEV

I doubt it. I can see further than you. I've had experience of life. I haven't given you the happiness that you hoped for! Perhaps, I'm too old. In ten years, in five years, possibly sooner, you will meet a man and you will say "Now there goes happiness passing by!" you understand that I will live in a perpetual agony, that I am going to prepare myself for the struggle—because I want to keep you, because I cling infinitely to you.

LAURA

But I will remain faithful. I intend to be happy with you, I will be.

POZNICHEV

Happy? I'd have to be really sick to believe it. (He moves away from her)

LAURA

(With passion) I will know how to persuade you.

POZNICHEV

It was necessary for your joy to be manifested, bursting out, superhuman. And yet I will ask myself where this joy comes from.

LAURA

You have no right to speak this way. You have no shame! (She weeps)

POZNICHEV

I beg your pardon—There—on my knees—Forget what I just said. It's the brute speaking in me.

LAURA

(Rising, eyes still wet) No—You see—It's over. (Servant enters)

SERVANT

(Announcing) Mr. Troukhasinsky!

LAURA

It's your friend, the musician. Are we going to receive

him?

POZNICHEV

It would be shameful to shut the door on him today, the day after our return.

LAURA

Still—

POZNICHEV

I don't wish to offend him. (To servant) Show him in. (The servant leaves)

POZNICHEV

(Going to Troukhasinsky) Hello, old boy Come, greet my wife. That's over. Now, listen to me. You've come at a bad moment. You're a great deal of wit, it's understood. Unfortunately, I warn you that anything you say today will appear to be an imbecility.

TROUKHASINSKY

Why in that case. (With a gesture towards the door)

POZNICHEV

I'm keeping you and I'm not letting you go. You see the piano is open. Sit down and play something. You come at a bad moment! Play! Play!

LAURA

Melancholy—

(Troukhasinsky begins playing *The Kreutzer Sonata*. Poznichev who is seated by Laura takes her hand then her waist)

POZNICHEV

(Low) You love me, right?

LAURA

(Evasive) Why yes—why yes—

POZNICHEV

Tell me you love me.

LAURA

Let me listen; it's so beautiful! He plays with so much soul.

POZNICHEV

Give me your lips. He cannot see us. (Laura leans softly in Poznichev's shoulder—he kisses her lips)

TROUKHASINSKY

(Stopping abruptly and looking at them) Well, this is pretty! Do you take me for a gypsy?

POZNICHEV

Don't be annoyed old boy. Play on!

CURTAIN

ACT TWO

Laura is holding her face in her hands half turned over on a sofa. Poznichev is beside her—He has neurotic gestures.

POZNICHEV

Look—Speak to me.

LAURA

What do you want me to say to you?

POZNICHEV

Never mind what—Don't stay like that. Our poor little one—even yesterday.

LAURA

Poznichev—why are they taking so long down there?

POZNICHEV

Don't be uneasy. When two doctors get together to

examine a sick person they talk for a half hour at least.

LAURA

But their consultation is lasting more than that.

POZNICHEV

(Pulling his watch out) Twenty-five minutes.

LAURA

Ah!

POZNICHEV

Here you are half crazy; that's the first result of the consultation.

LAURA

As for you, you're calm.

POZNICHEV

No—First of all, this consultation that you wanted—was it necessary?

LAURA

You aren't going to reproach me for worrying when the health of my child is at stake?

POZNICHEV

You worry yourself too much! For the least cold you move heaven and earth. If you heard my uncle!

LAURA

I have no confidence in him as a doctor.

POZNICHEV

Because he is my uncle.

LAURA

Because he is attached to old methods.

POZNICHEV

I assure you they are the same as those of Ivanoff, your favorite doctor.

LAURA

No.

POZNICHEV

What do you know about it? How can you judge of these things? (Laura shrugs her shoulders) What is it that pleases you about him? His eyes, his beard, his unctuous way of speaking. It's because he's young?

LAURA

What do you expect? He understands me.

POZNICHEV

Is it necessary to understand you to care for the throat of your daughter? The truth is that this doctor has insinuinated himself in our home.

LAURA

I call him when people are ill.

POZNICHEV

But he's been in the house since we had children. He flattered; he exalted your maternal feeling. I don't know what you would do, if, with his concurrence, you couldn't discover some malady in them.

LAURA

I assure you that Doctor Ivanoff has cared for our two children with admirable devotion.

POZNICHEV

And my uncle? Only look—from their birth doctor Ivanoff has imposed the noble task on you of weighing them before and after every meal.

LAURA

(Coldly) It's interesting.

POZNICHEV

(Continuing) And to say the whole thing, he's always of your opinion—he's your ally—he's the natural ally of all women.

LAURA

Under that pretext you've separated me from my old priest.

POZNICHEV

Let him return! (He walks agitatedly)

LAURA

In short, you are reproaching me for being too good a mother!

POZNICHEV

(Walks, agitated, then) No—come—hug me. (He moves back. The door opens. The Uncle and Ivanoff enter)

UNCLE

(Joyfully) Well, I was telling him that it's only an angina—

DOCTOR

(With a gesture of understanding to Laura) Pultaceous.

LAURA

If it's only an angina, why did you stay so long?

UNCLE

Dr. Ivanoff was explaining to me a communication he's going to make to the Academy of Medicine.

POZNICHEV

(Between his teeth) Oh! Indeed.

DOCTOR

(To Poznichev) On scarlet fever.

LAURA

(Excitedly) You were speaking of my children?

DOCTOR

Why certainly. This case was completely interesting.

LAURA

(To Poznichev) You see—

POZNICHEV

But they don't have scarlet fever.

UNCLE

That's my opinion.

DOCTOR

Ah, pardon! Pardon!

LAURA

What's this—you say—(All shout for a moment)

DOCTOR

(Dominating the uproar) Still, there was a discussion. You see plainly that the case was interesting.

(A pause)

LAURA

(Taking Ivanoff aside) It's an angina—Then what must be done?

UNCLE

(Who has heard) Nothing. Keep the children warm.

POZNICHEV

That's it—

DOCTOR

(Low) Keep the children warm. Employ my gargle—moreover I will prescribe a treatment—

POZNICHEV

Your gargle.

UNCLE

Do you think it's needed?

POZNICHEV

Let's not complicate things. What's the use of exhausting the child?

DOCTOR

It's the way I treated the daughter of Lénine, little Olga. She had such a grievous constitution.

POZNICHEV

But my daughter has a healthy nature—she is robust.

UNCLE

She's a tough kid, my niece.

DOCTOR

I don't think so.

LAURA

You hear.

POZNICHEV

My children aren't vigorous? Sacha, neither?

DOCTOR

Neither.

LAURA

I told you so indeed.

DOCTOR

It's rare than in a certain class the children are strong— Men marry late.

POZNICHEV

What's that mean—late?

DOCTOR

I mean by that, that before marrying they had abused all sorts of pleasures.

UNCLE

They are dangerous to the race—The pleasures of a bachelor—

DOCTOR

Like those of marriage. Think that in our country and also others, women are harassed by work and by love—until the day the child is born.

UNCLE

Bah! Do we know if excesses are still injurious to the race? Isn't precocity an effect of alcohol?—If your little daughter, Poznichev, exhibits so much taste for music, perhaps it's because one night you took a drop too much of Kummel.

DOCTOR

(Low to Laura) Metaphysician.

LAURA

Doesn't she have one of those extraordinary dispositions for music?

DOCTOR

Once again, yesterday, our friend Troukhasinsky said so.

LAURA

Truly. (To Poznichev) You hear.

POZNICHEV

Well—what?

LAURA

Doesn't that please you?

POZNICHEV

It's strange we can't speak of music without pronouncing Troukhasinsky's name.

LAURA

Why he's the only musician that we know.

POZNICHEV

That doesn't suffice—if I listened to you our house would become a box at the concert. Ah, doctor, there's yet another malady you must care for.

UNCLE

Love of music?

POZNICHEV

And musicians (Nervously) Still, I don't say that for Troukhasinsky.

DOCTOR

Charming man, isn't he?

POZNICHEV

Yes.

DOCTOR

He was the one who introduced me to you.

POZNICHEV

I will never forget it.

DOCTOR

(Looking at his watch) I'm going to write out my order. The child must follow a regime, take a tonic. (Gestures as if looking for something to write)

POZNICHEV

If you'd step into my office. (Ivanoff leaves)

UNCLE

As for me, I'm leaving you.

POZNICHEV

I beg you, Uncle—come see what he's going to write—

UNCLE

Ah, we'll be a quarter of an hour! He is so meticulous.

POZNICHEV

(Heading towards the exit) Come anyway. You heard him try to persuade my wife that I married her too late.

UNCLE

Why no.

LAURA

I am coming with you.

Servant

(Enters, announcing) Mr. Troukhasinsky.

POZNICHEV

Well—I will receive him—or well, no—stay here—that's the thing you receive him—No need to advise you to be friendly. (He gives a little laugh. Laura looks at him speechless)

TROUKHASINSKY

(Entering) Anya's doing well?

LAURA

Thanks to God!

TROUKHASINSKY

Ah! So much the better—here are some cough lozenges for her and these here—are for you. (He pulls a sheet of music from his pocket. He sighs.)

LAURA

Why are you sighing?

TROUKHASINSKY

First of all, sighing is the job of a musician.

LAURA

You know that my husband doesn't like your sighs.

TROUKHASINSKY

He doesn't like music. His prosaic soul often afflicts me.

LAURA

Look, why are you sighing, big baby?

TROUKHASINSKY

This waltz—this slow waltz, I wrote for you, for you alone. I ardently desire to dedicate it to you.

LAURA

And the prosaic soul of my husband is opposed to it?

TROUKHASINSKY

Still, it was you who inspired this music.

LAURA

My husband pretends that an honest woman doesn't

inspire music.

TROUKHASINSKY

Let's not talk about it anymore. Musicians know how to suffer in silence.

LAURA

They play.

TROUKHASINSKY

No—They have recourse to an artificial paradise. Because they find a way to forget.

LAURA

Are you going to speak to me about your morphine again?

TROUKHASINSKY

(Pulling a small flash from his pocket) It's a passion an Irish girl gave me.

LAURA

You inject the morphine?

TROUKHASINSKY

Not in the arm—because of my art.

LAURA

Often?

TROUKHASINSKY

Very often—for the last several months.

LAURA

Liar! It's pretty, your flask. Give it to me (She takes it) I am confiscating it. You are not angry?

TROUKHASINSKY

I am touched. (A pause) Why doesn't your husband want us to play four hands?

LAURA

Hell—Because of the pedals. (They laugh) This brave Poznichev!

TROUKHASINSKY

He's gone out?

LAURA

No, he's here, in the smoking room.

TROUKHASINSKY

(Low) Behind the door.

LAURA

(Holding her ear) No.

TROUKHASINSKY

He's atrociously jealous.

LAURA

A tiger.

TROUKHASINSKY

He's jealous of everybody.

LAURA

Of you especially!

TROUKHASINSKY

Of me? He does me too much honor.

LAURA

You are an artist, a virtuoso.

TROUKHASINSKY

The reputation of musicians is superficial. In the past I don't say no—But since the progress of aviation, our prestige has diminished.

LAURA

Hush, I hear steps.

TROUKHASINSKY

You are mistaken.

LAURA

Yes, yes—

TROUKHASINSKY

You are not pretending to have hearing more acute than mine?

LAURA

No, but I am accustomed. (The door opens)

TROUKHASINSKY

The tiger? (They laugh as Poznichev enters)

POZNICHEV

Hello, dear friend; I'd forgotten that you were here.

TROUKHASINSKY

Really?

POZNICHEV

(To Laura) He pays you his respects, Doctor Ivanoff.

TROUKHASINSKY

Ivanoff is here?

POZNICHEV

He just left. (Pause) Why were you laughing when I came in?

LAURA

He was telling me a story.

POZNICHEV

Tell it to me.

TROUKHASINSKY

Another time. Anecdotes lose their savor when they are repeated.

POZNICHEV

Before a husband.

LAURA

(To Troukhasinsky) Do him that pleasure, I beg you!

POZNICHEV

(grimacing) No! Was it smutty, his tale?

TROUKHASINSKY

Oh—can you imagine?

POZNICHEV

You don't know your profession—An anecdote must be spicy, crude, smutty to please the ladies. Especially avoid circumlocutions or to have success with your public, you must call things by their name—and when the thing has two names, choose without hesitation—the worst.

LAURA

You piss me off.

POZNICHEV

Offer them the text fearlessly—they will demand illustrations of you.

LAURA

(Violently) Will you shut up? Where do you get the right to speak to me in that way?

TROUKHASINSKY

If I came rather sooner than usual, it's by chance—

POZNICHEV

As for me, if I remained home, it's also by chance. Ah—chance!

TROUKHASINSKY

I like to think you are joking.

POZNICHEV

You've doubtless guessed I am joking.

LAURA

(Suddenly violent) What is it makes you suppose that?

POZNICHEV

What?

LAURA

By what right do you address such reproaches to me?

POZNICHEV

What reproaches? Go, your dressmaker is expecting you.

LAURA

(Holding back tears) Yes, I'm going. That will be better (Choked voice) You will wait for me, won't you, Mr. Troukhasinsky? I won't say goodbye.

POZNICHEV

Why you know that this brave Troukhasinsky can remain. You need time to try your dresses.

LAURA

(Looking at Troukhasinsky) No—I won't be long.

POZNICHEV

Troukhasinsky's not a man of leisure, he's a musician. It's indeed necessary for him to sit from time to time at a piano. Say goodbye to the gentleman.

LAURA

Goodbye. (She leaves hurriedly)

POZNICHEV

(Shrugging his shoulders) What a comedy.

TROUKHASINSKY

(Rising) Goodbye, sir.

POZNICHEV

My, my! A little *tête-à-tête* with me doesn't tempt you!

TROUKHASINSKY

You've made me understand in a very polite way that my presence was inopportune; a musician must seat himself from time to time before a piano.

POZNICHEV

(Raising his head) Stay, will you? We have to talk.

TROUKHASINSKY

About what?

POZNICHEV

(With a forced smile) Of generalities, dear sir, of generalities, naturally. With men like you is it possible to speak otherwise? You are sitting (Troukhasinsky is undecided) Then make a decision. You don't like philosophy by chance? You'd really be wrong. Philosophy is a beautiful thing, sir.

TROUKHASINSKY

(Harshly) I don't doubt it.

POZNICHEV

(With a forced laugh) A fine thing. So, you are speaking calmly of abstractions, of nebulous things, far off, that you think have no connection with your personal existence, and suddenly, and suddenly it seems to you that these distant things are the same as those that obsess you, that you see in nightmares, which awaken you at night. As for me, I love this sensation.

TROUKHASINSKY

You are an esthete—I always suspected it.

POZNICHEV

You're staying?

TROUKHASINSKY

(Throwing his hat on the table) So be it!

POZNICHEV

I knew that you would remain. I am happy to have a good conversation like we used to. You've been wrong to neglect me. Since I got married you've detached yourself from me. It's true that my wife never leaves us alone.

TROUKHASINSKY

I took a tour for two years in America—one gets lost from view. Look, we're still close. What separates folks is time and space.

POZNICHEV

Still, despite time and space—you still take an interest in my wife—Whereas for me—Look it's villainous to neglect an old friend like me for a new friendship. I am bothered by it. As for me, I'm very jealous.

TROUKHASINSKY

We've been close for so long that we no longer have

important things to tell each other.

POZNICHEV

Very natural, assuredly—it's not very natural; only if you'd taken the trouble to observe me you would have known that I've changed greatly.

TROUKHASINSKY

Really?

POZNICHEV

Why yes, since I married I've become a completely unusual type. (With a smile) Me too, I deserve to be studied. Heavens, why we are standing—will you sit down. (Gesture by Troukhasinsky) No, not there—There, there (Pointing to a seat by the table) We will put out this light over here and light this one. (Lights a lamp on the table) Now, let's sit side by side (They sit) You're comfortable.

TROUKHASINSKY

Very comfortable, thanks.

POZNICHEV

Now we're going to speak privately. (They look at each other) You know if one of us lies; the other one will divine it right away from his face.

TROUKHASINSKY

I have no intention of lying.

POZNICHEV

Certainly. Certainly. Do you know what must be done to know if a woman lies? You can guess nothing from her face—absolutely nothing—they are more malign than we are. Do you know what must be done?

TROUKHASINSKY

(with hate) No.

POZNICHEV

When you get married you will learn. You mustn't make anything of a woman's words, for her speech will always be correct, nor look at her eyes because they are obscured by a semblance of tears. If you want to know the truth, close your eyes and listen to her voice—and one fine day her intonation will give a very clear impression to you—The certitude you are a cuckold. Charming isn't it?

TROUKHASINSKY

(Nervous) I'm deuced! I'm deuced! (Poznichev lowers his eyes, a brief silence then he resumes)

POZNICHEV

They tell me that you had great success with women last year in New York. Is it true?

TROUKHASINSKY

Thanks. I'm not complaining.

POZNICHEV

Your vogue has not diminished since.

TROUKHASINSKY

Nothing!

POZNICHEV

You astonish me.

TROUKHASINSKY

You think I'm in decline?

POZNICHEV

No, surely. It's your frankness that astonishes me.

TROUKHASINSKY

You're funny, you are! Why should I hide from your successes that everybody knows of?

POZNICHEV

There they don't hide these things from the husband?

TROUKHASINSKY

(Cocking his head) From the husband? Of whom are you speaking? I don't understand you.

POZNICHEV

Really? (A pause) There's something I want to know—a title purely documentary—my question will perhaps be a bit indiscreet.

TROUKHASINSKY

Don't trouble yourself. You're not used to it.

POZNICHEV

Among the women you're loved—The greatest number were married?

TROUKHASINSKY

Right.

POZNICHEV

But those who were mothers didn't succumb as easily, as quickly as the others, right? And then, you found them naturally less seductive. I am sure that in your collection, mothers were rare exceptions—

TROUKHASINSKY

Oh, no!

POZNICHEV

No? But then—they were distracted, hysterical, neurotics, they weren't wives such as one meets every day at every step, right?

TROUKHASINSKY

Neurotics? Hysterics? Why, I wouldn't want them. They were very ordinary women.

POZNICHEV

But then, they had singular husbands—Their husbands were, weren't they?

TROUKHASINSKY

There were blondes and brunettes.

POZNICHEV

Were they old, ugly, nasty, stupid, hunchedback?

TROUKHASINSKY

Hunchbacked—Oh, no I wouldn't have wanted that—They were very ordinary men.

POZNICHEV

Like you and me—

TROUKHASINSKY

Like—me—

POZNICHEV

How is it they didn't see the danger —? For still, an honest woman doesn't fall into the arms of a gentleman from one day to the next; there must be preambles—methods of approach—time—

TROUKHASINSKY

Yes—lots of time.

POZNICHEV

Right! The fools! The fools! For, in the end, they see quite clearly when a man pays court to a woman and she begins to give in to his solicitations. That jumps out, you cannot mistake it.

TROUKHASINSKY

Right.

POZNICHEV

An intelligent man stops his wife before the fall—offers her his hand—defends her against herself.

TROUKHASINSKY

Are you really sure of that?

POZNICHEV

A woman can—

TROUKHASINSKY

What? If a woman is not honest, she falls fatally. The vigilance of the husband will do nothing.

POZNICHEV

And if the wife is honest?

TROUKHASINSKY

She will know how to protect herself.

POZNICHEV

(Ironic) She'll know? Then the husband can sleep

undisturbed?

TROUKHASINSKY

He would do well.

POZNICHEV

You would really like to see me adopt your theory? It's handy—for you—

TROUKHASINSKY

For everybody—believe in my experience.

POZNICHEV

Nothing can guarantee the fidelity of a woman.

TROUKHASINSKY

If she's not in love—nothing.

POZNICHEV

But how to tell if a woman loves you? Do you know?

TROUKHASINSKY

Certainly.

POZNICHEV

What do you do to make women love you? (He looks at him for a long time)

TROUKHASINSKY

They find me sweet, sincere—

POZNICHEV

In what does your charm consist? What do you do that they run after you?

TROUKHASINSKY

Nothing extraordinary.

POZNICHEV

You've never asked yourself why these unfortunates fall precisely in your arms and not in those of your servant?

TROUKHASINSKY

(Modestly) Social conventions—

POZNICHEV

Not at all. Why your music.

TROUKHASINSKY

Yes, my music if you insist.

POZNICHEV

The fine art, the noble diversion that is your music! A gentleman in full dress sits before a piano. His fingers have hardly touched the keyboard before the irreproachable mothers, the modest wives are dreaming. Have you ever thought what these irreproachable mothers can be thinking of?

TROUKHASINSKY

Of an ideal of beauty, I suppose.

POZNICHEV

Of an ideal of pleasure! Hush! They dream of a distant land where one is satiated without having eaten, where one reposes without having worked, where the climate is eternally warm, where delight is without sorrow, where pleasure is without effort, joy without cause, and love without exhaustion, without sin, without children—That's what it is—beauty—

TROUKHASINSKY

I am conscious of giving a small ideal—that suffices.

POZNICHEV

You give the ideal? Let's talk about that! But the dope dealer gives it also, and the peddler who sells students obscene cards equally gives the ideal—and the same as you!

TROUKHASINSKY

Let's distinguish.

POZNICHEV

(Interrupting him) Do you know what I would do to my wife if she abandoned herself to your ideal, if like the others, she confounded love of music with love of musicians, do you know what I would do? I wouldn't touch the man—

TROUKHASINSKY

Yes—They say that first and then strike—

POZNICHEV

The lover—I'd let him flee—for he had promised me nothing. In trying his seductions on my wife, he was in his role:—if a man approaches her it's with the idea of taking her. I know it and I have only to be on my guard. But the woman—do you know what I would do—? (A pause) I would kill her!

TROUKHASINSKY

You won't do it.

POZNICHEV

I will kill her! I will kill her!

TROUKHASINSKY

You are mad! You are mad! (They rise. Poznichev is the first to sit down)

POZNICHEV

(With a forced laugh) I really told you that philosophy was an interesting thing! How it warms up, sometimes, in speaking of distant matters of improbable conjectures. Is it strange enough? (Changing tone) But we've understood, each other. You'd like my wife and I intend to keep her.

TROUKHASINSKY

Look, this is crazy. Your wife is honest.

POZNICHEV

You're not the judge of that! Leave.

TROUKHASINSKY

Huh?

POZNICHEV

Leave—With people of your ilk, musicians, strolling players, mountebanks, you must explain things clearly. Leave and never come back. I don't wish my wife to see you. I forbid you to address a word to her even in public. If you meet her at a party—you would do well to avoid her—if not— (Threatening gesture)

TROUKHASINSKY

You are saying? (Then, controlling himself) I'm giving you time to retract your words. I do it in memory of our former friendships.

POZNICHEV

As for me—I've forgotten everything.

TROUKHASINSKY

You appear to me to have lost your common sense.

POZNICHEV

That's no concern of yours.

TROUKHASINSKY

I've been friendly towards your wife—but as towards all women—without thinking of evil.

POZNICHEV

Without thinking of evil? You? Then you think I'm very naïve. I hear my wife coming. I forbid you to speak to her. Leave. (Troukhasinsky shrugs his shoulder and leaves)

LAURA

(Enters and looks about as if she were seeking someone) Ah!

POZNICHEV

He left.

LAURA

He didn't wait for me?

POZNICHEV

You see. You're vexed? That'll teach you to beg gentlemen to wait for you. This poor Troukhasinsky doubtless had a rendezvous—

LAURA

What do you know about it?

POZNICHEV

I know what I know, but my poor girl, he's laughing at you like other women. I had a discussion with him. I pity his mistresses. Can you imagine—he told me everything—he gave me names, many names. Truly he lacks delicacy.

LAURA

Names?

POZNICHEV

Why yes—he would really be wrong to trouble himself—A woman who deceives her husband is only a—you know indeed what—

LAURA

You repeat it often enough.

POZNICHEV

You understand that between men one tells everything.

LAURA

That's pretty.

POZNICHEV

It's only in novels that a sin remains hidden. In life, everything is known—Everybody is *au courant* of a liaison.

LAURA

Except the husband, right? (Poznichev starts) You are vexed?

POZNICHEV

Vexed by what?

LAURA

(Laughing nervously) You said he gave you names.

POZNICHEV

Precisely.

LAURA

What names?

POZNICHEV

(Embarrassed) Don't dwell on it,—as for me, I am not a lover—I have some delicacy—

LAURA

At least you don't know how to lie.

POZNICHEV

Yes, it's true I don't know how to lie, but you—

LAURA

But me?

POZNICHEV

As for you, you never lie, do you? In that case, tell me, why'd you want him to stay? What did you have to tell him that was so urgent? Heavens—ink stains on your fingers. What did you write—a note and for him. You have it in your pocket—Give me— (He makes a gesture of seizing it)

LAURA

You are absurd. Are you going to search me? (Turning out her pockets) There—are you satisfied?

POZNICHEV

I was wrong—let's make peace—kiss me.

LAURA

You bore me, you bore me.

POZNICHEV

Yes—you need to be amused, I bore you—I've known it for a long while.

LAURA

I am as indifferent to your brutality as to your caresses.

POZNICHEV

And yet you submit to them.

LAURA

Oh! My God!

POZNICHEV

You'd indeed like to rid yourself of me. That's all you think about. When you go to a card reader, it's to ask her if you'll soon be a widow.

LAURA

(Terrified) Poznichev—What's that you're saying?

POZNICHEV

If this continues much longer, I'll be afraid to eat and drink here; if this continues anything is possible.

LAURA

Treat me like a prisoner right away!

POZNICHEV

To whom were you writing?

LAURA

I simply signed a receipt.

POZNICHEV

And it's by writing one word that you stained your fingers like this? You intend to make me believe that?

LAURA

(Outraged) The pen didn't work!

POZNICHEV

I will verify that.

LAURA

Go, verify it.

POZNICHEV

Later. (A pause) So, really, the musician is indifferent to you?

LAURA

Absolutely indifferent.

POZNICHEV

(Observing) Very good. I suspected it and I just kicked him out.

LAURA

You did that?

POZNICHEV

Why yes—

LAURA

(Voice trembling) A friend!

POZNICHEV

Yes, a friend—which proves I've got serious reasons.

LAURA

(Violently) I know what they are, your reasons! If you think it's clever what you just did—That that will prevent me—

POZNICHEV

From seeing him? Why certainly, my little one, that will prevent you. This musician has an elite soul. That's understood, but he's a prudent man. I indicated to him that if I were ever to see you talking together, he will have business with me. Be calm, he will flee you, and he'll be wise to do so.

LAURA

(Dolorous) So, it's true, you kicked him out—like the others.

POZNICHEV

Exactly—like the others. But why make so much fuss over someone who's indifferent.

LAURA

(Fainting in an armchair) I am sad—I am sad.

POZNICHEV

(With a little sweetness) Tell me, it's because I separated you from your musician that you are sad?

LAURA

(Doleful) No, it's your house that's sad, at my mother's I never heard a harsh word, an insult. Everybody loved me. And now what awaits me? You haven't beaten me yet—but perhaps you are going to do it. You frighten me—but this I won't bear—I will never bear it.

POZNICHEV

Laura, my poor Laura, don't speak to me this way, you hurt me, I suffer.

LAURA

And you, haven't you hurt me? Nasty! Nasty!

POZNICHEV

You know quite well I'm not bad.

LAURA

(Shaking her head) When you get angry—

POZNICHEV

I won't get angry anymore. I put up with everything on your part, scenes, reproaches, tears. All I want is to believe you. I have confidence in you. Would you like to kiss me?

LAURA

I'd like to very much.

POZNICHEV

Now, give me your hand, your poor little hand, give it to me so I can kiss it. (Putting her hand to his lips) Again. (Changed voice) Heavens, that stain—still I have confidence—you can tell me who you wrote to.

LAURA

(Despairing) Poznichev! Poznichev! (A pause)

POZNICHEV

(Recoiling with a gesture of discouragement) You must despise me—but this is stronger than I am!

LAURA

Already, already, finish. Yes, I see in your eyes you no longer believe me.

POZNICHEV

Yes, indeed—yes, indeed—If I only listened to my heart I would never conceive the least suspicion. Only my mind tells me otherwise, it tells me (He stops, perplexed)

LAURA

Speak, Poznichev your heart will be less heavy when you've confided your pain to me—Come, sit down, near me. What does your mind say? (He sits near her)

POZNICHEV

It says to me: "Watch your wife more than a thief. She hasn't yet deceived you—but that proves nothing." And despite myself I see a bundle of arguments, of probabilities, of memories rise up. It's stronger than I am!

LAURA

Speak! Speak! Since this idea is torturing you, do you want us to work together to destroy it? Come on, don't turn away from me. You are going to see, I am going to cure you. (Poznichev hides his face in his hands. He seems to weep)

LAURA

Don't weep when I tell you I am going to cure you. (Caressing his hair) What makes you think I would be unfaithful? (Poznichev is mute) Come on, when did you conceive a suspicion for the first time? Was it long ago?

POZNICHEV

(In a very uneasy voice) Yes.

LAURA

After our honeymoon?

POZNICHEV

Yes, I believe that was when—Yes, it was when I realized you'd never been happy in my arms—that I said to myself—Heavens—She lied for three months.

LAURA

But if I lied, it was so as not to hurt you.

POZNICHEV

Evidently that's one explanation. But I thought—She's really good at it, she lies well. Then the idea came to me that were you to meet a younger man who knew how to make himself loved by you—you would give yourself to him in complete security because you know how to lie.

LAURA

(Taking his head) You must listen to me, do what I tell you. Will you listen to me?

POZNICHEV

Yes.

LAURA

To begin—get it in your head that there are many honest women—many more than you believe.

POZNICHEV

(Docilely) Yes—

LAURA

Even in our class—First of all there's your mother—(A pause) And mine—

POZNICHEV

(With a side glance) Huh!

LAURA

You said?

POZNICHEV

Nothing—Continue.

LAURA

And then if you weren't idle you wouldn't have time to

analyze, to dispute, to suspect from morn to midnight. What you need is regular work to occupy your mind—a work that's absorbing and not too difficult. I don't want to exhaust you.

POZNICHEV

It's been so long since I've worked.

LAURA

You're too much of a homebody, you ought from time to time to take trips in Russia and to foreign countries—business trips, so you won't get bored too much. Sometimes you need to change the air. An honorable, easy position—is there nothing which could tempt you?

POZNICHEV

Indeed that's what I need.

LAURA

Well, you will find it. But you can't always be traveling. It would be good to make our house more gay. You will be content to hear laughing when you come home, right?

POZNICHEV

Certainly.

LAURA

You must get back together with some friends that you've unjustly offended so as to renew former relationships. It won't be difficult, go! All you'll have to do is to give a nice greeting to each one. (Taking his head) And that poor musician you treated so pitilessly—you will write him a nice word, right? (Kissing him)

POZNICHEV

I'm going to follow your advice (Laura looks at him, astonished)

POZNICHEV

You want a change of air? Well, we'll both change it together. We'll go live in the country. That's okay with you?

LAURA

So be it.

POZNICHEV

You are thinking doubtless that I'm speaking of my country-place in the neighborhood of Saint Petersburg, where there's music. Well, no, undeceive yourself. That won't change the air for us enough. I intend to go into the depths of Russia—Three hundred kilometers from the railway, five hundred kilometers from the nearest village. What do you think of that?

LAURA

You will always be the same. Your jealousy, your nastiness will follow you everywhere. And then, down there, like here, there are men.

POZNICHEV

Peasants. I promise you that the first who raises his eyes to you will die under the knout. Go, I am going to be calm.

LAURA

I'm not going.

POZNICHEV

Huh?

LAURA

I don't wish to go.

POZNICHEV

You don't wish to go, I think I'm the boss.

LAURA

You wouldn't drag me by force?

POZNICHEV

And what do you know about it?

LAURA

I don't wish to be buried alone!

POZNICHEV

(With an evil laugh) You—will be with me—What more do you want?

LAURA

(With terror) I'm afraid of you. I know you. The whole day you'll run through the fields, at night, you'll come home worn out, wild, with the blood of a stag on your hands. You'll start your endless interrogatories and your inquests—You will make me die of terror, is that what you want?

POZNICHEV

You must have very strong attachments here, to complain with such heat.

LAURA

I cling to my friends—to those who remain to me.

POZNICHEV

They displease me.

LAURA

Here I have my family, my mother, you won't separate me from them, I think.

POZNICHEV

She can only give you bad advice.

LAURA

I won't go.

POZNICHEV

Don't force me to use violence; you know I'll use it. I won't trouble about that.

LAURA

I will escape on the first occasion I see an open door.

POZNICHEV

And so as for me, I will have you brought you back by

the police.

LAURA

Wretch! I cannot live with you. I hate you. There's only one way for me to escape, But I will use it. You'll have what you wish, murderer! (She leaves by the door at the left and locks it after her)

POZNICHEV

(After assuring himself that the door is actually locked) What a comedy! My God—What's the good of this comedy? (He walks around the room cracking his knuckles. Suddenly, we hear Laura's voice)

LAURA'S VOICE

George! George!

POZNICHEV

What's wrong?

LAURA'S VOICE

Open the door.

POZNICHEV

How do you expect me to go? The key's on your side.

LAURA'S VOICE

Break it down, quick.

POZNICHEV

And why can't you open it?

LAURA'S VOICE

I've poisoned myself.

POZNICHEV

(Between his teeth) Why's that? What a comedy!

LAURA'S VOICE

I'm ill! I'm ill!

POZNICHEV

(Between his teeth) Lie! Lie! (Noise of a chair can be heard) Now the furniture. (A profound silence) Why, I no longer hear anything. It was true, true! (He shakes the door) Laura! Laura! (He rings. To servant who appears) The door—Quickly—Let's break it down—A disaster has occurred.

CURTAIN

ACT THREE

Vera is preparing a potion. Poznichev is crumpled up in an armchair; he seems drowsy. Mother is near Vera.

MOTHER

(To Vera) Twist—Twist.

VERA

It's taking a long while to melt.

MOTHER

Harder. Courage.

VERA

No, decidedly, Mama, I can't do anymore.

MOTHER

Rest—You look exhausted.

VERA

Here it is three days I've watched. I'm not used to it.

MOTHER

(Pointing to Poznichev) You think perhaps this gentleman watched? As for him, he doesn't take things easy. God be praised, he puts up with it well. You see he hasn't budged from his armchair. The gentleman is resting—his wife has been inches from death—he sleeps—that's the limit! He sleeps.

VERA

I really think he's broken.

MOTHER

(To Vera) Sit down. (To Poznichev) Get up, Vera wants to sit down. Go sleep somewhere else; at least you won't be disturbing anyone. (Poznichev rises and goes to another armchair. Vera sits in his place) Look at him—look at that head for me. Truly, he doesn't care. What's he seem like?

VERA

Look, Mother, leave him alone.

MOTHER

Did he leave my daughter alone? For whole years he took pleasure in torturing her. It amused him to make her suffer. Children aren't so cruel to animals. And, she, poor thing, who let him do it—who never said a word to me. Because if I knew—things would have happened differently!

VERA

He's repenting.

MOTHER

He's repenting? In what do you see that? Another man, in his place would tear his hair out in despair. Have you seen a single tear fall from his eyes? When I think that the servants were weeping. I am so ashamed for him.

VERA

It's true he hasn't wept.

MOTHER

He did everything he could to drive her to suicide; he thought no one would save her, that he would cheaply rid himself of his wife, the murderer!

VERA

Come on, Mama, you are exaggerating.

MOTHER

Go, I know him.

VERA

Why if you knew him, why didn't you intervene sooner?

MOTHER

I reproach myself for it, indeed, only this time it's really over, no he will never be able to terrorize her, or torture her again. If she's cured I will take her away forever. (Poznichev groans) You hear? The gentleman isn't happy that his toy will be taken from him, that a limit will be placed on his ferocity. What a beautiful soul!

VERA

Leave him alone!

MOTHER

You're right, I am making myself ill by thinking of this wretch. (Change of tone) The potion must be ready. (Going to the table and taking the cup) I'm going to take it to her. (She starts to leave and almost bumps into the armchair where Poznichev is seated)

MOTHER

(To Poznichev) As for you, you have a talent for annoying people! No one can pass without you threatening them. You do it deliberately. If you don't want to have your wife cared for at home, say so plainly and I'll take her to my place. (Poznichev goes to sit on a sofa, Mother leaves)

POZNICHEV

(Fearful) Vera! (A pause) Vera, if I speak to you, would you answer me? (A silence) You understand I'm kept in quarantine, I'm avoided—even the servants look at me with disdain—Still, I need to talk—

VERA

You have something to ask of me?

POZNICHEV

Yes, yes—You are good—Yes, very good—Like Laura. Laura has her faults, perhaps, but I think she's good and sweet—I think that. Isn't that your opinion?

VERA

Why, certainly!

POZNICHEV

I don't know why the idea came to me—Perhaps it is because of your sweetness—That you were going to take my side—defend me.

VERA

Against whom? (Poznichev makes an embarrassed gesture) No, don't count on that.

POZNICHEV

I'm expressing myself badly—evidently that would be asking too much of you. But can I hope on your part for a little benevolence, some sympathy.

VERA

Hurry up—what have you got to tell me?

POZNICHEV

First of all, how's Laura doing?

VERA

She's getting better. The doctor just said so.

POZNICHEV

Thank God! Thank God! (A pause) Tell me, Vera, is it

true, they're going to separate her from me, is it true your mother is seriously thinking of taking her away with her forever?—Or indeed did she say it only to frighten me? (With anguish) Is it really decided?

VERA

Nothing's been decided yet.

POZNICHEV

(With anguish) But they're going to talk about it?

VERA

Have you at least experienced a little regret, a little repentance?

POZNICHEV

(Embarrassed) Surely—but not as much as I would have wished. One thought preoccupies me—a problem—Your mother said just now I was sleeping: That's a mistake if I was closing my eyes, it was to regroup my memories to replay the drama, to find the decisive detail, to grasp the truth which is escaping me—

VERA

The truth which is escaping you?

POZNICHEV

You don't understand?

VERA

(Astonished at Poznichev's tone) Truly, no—you are a strange man. (The door opens giving entry to the Doctor Ivanoff)

DOCTOR

I have the pleasure of announcing to you that she is saved. The cure is complete. (To Vera) Your mother wants to you help her to dress your sister.

VERA

What, Laura's getting up?

POZNICHEV

Already, so quickly?

DOCTOR

Yes, indeed, yes, indeed.

VERA

Bye, Doctor, till later. (She leaves)

DOCTOR

(To Poznichev) It happens that your wife is expressing the wish to see you today.

POZNICHEV

She is?

DOCTOR

I'm not opposed to that interview on one condition however—you will use great delicacy with her.

POZNICHEV

(Interrupting him) Doctor, you are an honest man. I'd like to pose a question to you. Be sincere—

DOCTOR

Why, sir—

POZNICHEV

Don't get angry, Doctor. You understand that for me this is a question of great, of capital importance. My whole life depends upon it.

DOCTOR

Aren't you exaggerating?

POZNICHEV

No. You are perhaps the only man who can dispel my doubts—

DOCTOR

What's it all about?

POZNICHEV

My wife poisoned herself with morphine.

DOCTOR

Precisely.

POZNICHEV

To what circumstance do you attribute her cure?

DOCTOR

To my treatment.

POZNICHEV

And besides that?

DOCTOR

The dose she absorbed was weak.

POZNICHEV

(Triumphant) Insufficient to kill her. She was never in danger of death.

DOCTOR

As to that—I don't assert that—I am unaware—(Poznichev makes a gesture of discouragement)

POZNICHEV

Yet one more question, Doctor. The action of morphine is swift.

DOCTOR

The symptoms appear after four minutes.

POZNICHEV

(Excitedly) Not sooner.

DOCTOR

Rarely.

POZNICHEV

"Rarely." Now there's a fine word to cover ignorance, a word which opens the door to every supposition.

DOCTOR

But why this interrogation?

POZNICHEV

(Going towards the door then returning) Answer me quickly with a yes or a no. My wife—did she really intend to kill herself or was it indeed only a comedy?

DOCTOR

A comedy!

POZNICHEV

Yes or no?

DOCTOR

Truly, I don't know how to reply to you. You see me baffled.

POZNICHEV

You weren't expecting this question?

DOCTOR

(Sincerely) No.

POZNICHEV

And you know?

DOCTOR

But what is it makes you suspect your wife was not sincere?

POZNICHEV

I have indications—a bit vague, it's true—

DOCTOR

For what purpose would she play a comedy?—What interest did she have?

POZNICHEV

What interest did she have? Why you know, sir, that now she is free to do what she pleases—She's the boss. That's nothing, is it? Now, I am no longer anything here. They laugh at me with impunity. Her mother insults me at every opportunity—I am a murderer. If all that were only for indigestion.

DOCTOR

What you are saying is monstrous.

POZNICHEV

Mother, Daughter, Sister can demand anything from me. And if I budge, if I make a resisting face—Laura comes forward weeping and threatening, a flask in her hand—and naturally, I will give in—And you know, in the flask—there will be nothing.

DOCTOR

There was poison in it, sir.

POZNICHEV

Ah, if she truly had suicidal ideas—If I were sure of it, I would correct myself. If I knew that only for an instant she was in danger of death—I would resign myself—But I don't have that certitude I can't tell you Doctor, what's taking place in me. It seems to me that I am a man they are plundering with impunity in broad daylight someone very strong, succumbing to someone very weak. I have no choice but to obey.

DOCTOR

But, still, tell me what makes you suspect the sincerity of your wife?

POZNICHEV

She isn't dead! If one truly intends to kill oneself—one—

DOCTOR

One dies?

POZNICHEV

I understand, perfectly, when one—with a firearm the hand trembles; but poison?

DOCTOR

The hand trembled pouring the poison that's all.

POZNICHEV

And then—there's something else—

DOCTOR

What's that?

POZNICHEV

When she went out saying she was going to kill herself, I was in this room—by the table. I remember exactly I twice walked around the room, then I took a newspaper. Indeed here it is—and I read this—I hadn't finished when I heard her cries. I am sure that only two minutes had elapsed—you said that it requires four.

DOCTOR

Sometimes the action of the poison is more rapid.

POZNICHEV

And she screamed to me. She called me. Do you know what would have happened if I hadn't broken down the door?

DOCTOR

What?

POZNICHEV

I would have caught my wife *in flagrante*, in a lie. She would have opened, herself, the door. But I am too sensitive for my own good. I broke down the door.

DOCTOR

And that's all. You don't have any other proof?

POZNICHEV

No.

DOCTOR

And you conclude?

POZNICHEV

I'm not concluding yet. But if my wife consents to remain with me nothing will be able to prevent me from thinking that she was putting on an act. If she truly wanted to kill herself, she would have.

DOCTOR

Under these circumstances I can only advise you to do one thing, separate from your wife. It would be dangerous for you both to prolong this common life.

POZNICHEV

That's not your concern.

DOCTOR

Evidently.

POZNICHEV

I understand. They asked you to speak to me in this way?

DOCTOR

Not at all. Goodbye!

POZNICHEV

Yet another word. You understand how private this conversation is and I don't need to ask your discretion.

DOCTOR

Professional secret.

POZNICHEV

And you won't give any advice to my wife—

DOCTOR

I am not a lawyer—Goodbye.

POZNICHEV

Ah, yes—There are lawyers, too. (The Doctor leaves. Poznichev is alone for a moment. The Mother enters)

MOTHER

Laura wants to come here. (Poznichev is silent) You hear? Laura's coming here. (Poznichev is silent)

POZNICHEV

Then what?

MOTHER

Then—get out of here. (Poznichev remains motionless for a moment then leaves. Laura enters leaning on Vera)

MOTHER

(To Laura) Heavens, sit there, my little one. You're not exhausted?

LAURA

No—You spoke to him really harshly.

MOTHER

He deserves it, my darling.

LAURA

Why did you send him away?

MOTHER

I was afraid that his presence would be disagreeable to you.

LAURA

I wanted to speak to him.

MOTHER

But first of all, you must know what you are going to tell him. Only—do you know?

LAURA

No—Not exactly.

MOTHER

Then, consider.

LAURA

Why, Mama, I think it's very simple. I am leaving with you—I'm taking my children. I will tell him I am leaving him without regret but also, without hate!

MOTHER

There you go. You are taking your children. Will he agree to it? He will want to keep his son.

VERA

He adores Sacha.

LAURA

We shall see.

MOTHER

And you, Vera, what do you think about it?

VERA

I think that at all costs, even renouncing her son, Laura must leave.

MOTHER

I have the impression he will make every concession, every sacrifice to convince you to remain with him.

VERA

(To Laura) Yes—Still, in your place, I would refuse.

MOTHER

I beg you, Vera. You are much too young to give your advice so bluntly.

VERA

But Mama, just now, you said in front of him that you were determined to take Laura with you.

MOTHER

In front of him!

LAURA

You still don't want me to resume living with him.

MOTHER

My intervention must be extremely discreet. I am begging you only to examine the pros and cons before making a decision.

LAURA

But Mama, you know quite well what my life is here!

MOTHER

It's going to change, I'll answer for that.

LAURA

Poznichev hasn't changed his character in three days.

MOTHER

Yes, but the situation is no longer the same. There's nothing stronger than a bull, and yet when you put a ring in his nose, a child could lead him.

LAURA

What I want is calm.

MOTHER

But you will have it, your calm—He's going to obey you like a small child.

LAURA

When I think of all that I've endured I don't want to begin over again.

MOTHER

Why, precisely it's for that you receive the benefits of your sufferings. Think of the enormous advantages, unique to your situation. You will do whatever you like. How much would you have given once to obtain these advantages? And now that you have them, you want to renounce them!

LAURA

He scares me!

MOTHER

Look—Look, evidently your husband hasn't been a model husband. He hasn't even always been correct to us—I've never found a son in him. I know indeed that sympathies can't be ordered. Why our poor Vera, if he'd had fraternal feelings for her, with his fortune, he would have been able to find a husband for her.

VERA

I beg you don't bring me into the discussion.

MOTHER

(Continuing) Now you can do anything you like with him. If you want to, he would think of the future of your sister.

VERA

I am of the opinion Laura ought to leave her husband and as soon as possible!

LAURA

But how could I be happy with a man who drove me to suicide?

MOTHER

To suicide?

VERA

But she almost died.

MOTHER

In the end she was saved.

LAURA

He hesitated to bring me help.

MOTHER

How do you know that?

LAURA

He didn't reply to my first call—And he was there—I heard him!

MOTHER

You were so cool?

LAURA

He wanted my death.

MOTHER

Still, he helped you.

LAURA

For a few moments he wanted my death. I cannot remain with him. He frightens me. Even his tenderness is terrible when he pulls me in his arms they close on me like a vice. Oh, his arms! His arms!

MOTHER

You were dreaming.

LAURA

I want to leave.

MOTHER

It is inadmissible that a feverish vision should separate you from your husband and your children!

LAURA

I am taking my daughter!

MOTHER

But you must leave him the boy.

LAURA

(on edge) What does it matter!

MOTHER

Think, Laura, that you are leaving, your child in the hands of a bizarre, fantastic man. Do you even know what he's going to do with him? Is he capable of raising a child?

LAURA

Alas!

MOTHER

Do you want your son to reproach you later for having abandoned him as if he wasn't yours, as if he didn't have the same right to your tenderness as his sister?

LAURA

(Nervously) Enough! Enough! I've understood. (A pause) So you'll be at ease having me with him?

MOTHER

What do you fear?

LAURA

Nothing. (To Vera) Call him.

MOTHER

You are a good—a reasonable child—kiss me! (Gesture by Laura)

MOTHER

You don't want to?

LAURA

No—later—

MOTHER

I am only thinking of your good. You don't wish to kiss me?

LAURA

(Bending towards her) If you insist on it.

MOTHER

My little one, my dear little one. I'll call him. (She leaves)

VERA

Laura, you are wrong—You mustn't give in.

LAURA

(Pulling Vera to her) I know it; I know it.

VERA

There's still time to leave. I beg you—think only of yourself.

LAURA

We mustn't be selfish; our parents always taught us that.

VERA

But, in a few months, if you see that life is unbearable—you will come find us.

LAURA

It will be too late. (She hides her face in her hands)

MOTHER

(Entering followed by Poznichev) (Low to Poznichev) Especially try to be likable.

POZNICHEV

(Squinting) The curtains of the room were lowered—I am blinded by the light. (Finding Laura with his eyes) Hello, Laura.

LAURA

Hello, Poznichev—Sit down.

POZNICHEV

Thanks. (He sits) How are you?

LAURA

Better—you've grown thin.

POZNICHEV

You, too—you are more lovely than the first day I met you.

VERA

It might have been better for you not to have known her.

POZNICHEV

Yes, perhaps it would have been better.

VERA

(To Laura) You hear him?

POZNICHEV

Better for her—for her—of course.

MOTHER

(To Poznichev and to Laura) Look, my children, don't look like this. Come closer. Despite all the wrongs you've done her—Laura really wants to forget—You hear, Poznichev?

POZNICHEV

She forgets? She is beauty, she is generosity itself. I knew it; I knew it.

MOTHER

Look, Poznichev—You can see she is ready to grant you your pardon. You have only to ask for it—

POZNICHEV

Laura I ask your pardon. I've been bad—so bad that I drove you to suicide—for its proven that you wanted to kill yourself!

VERA

You would do better not to remind her of her act of despair!

POZNICHEV

You're mistaken. This act of despair must be recalled—Nothing can overwhelm me more surely.

MOTHER

Truly, Poznichev you're giving proof of ill will. You don't find a word of regret, not one word of gratitude.

POZNICHEV

I thank you, Laura, for indeed wanting to remain here with me and not abandoning our home—

MOTHER

Right—continue.

POZNICHEV

I am rejoiced over it; but I'd like to pose a question to you. What is this reason that convinced you to remain with me?

LAURA

My children!

POZNICHEV

(Waiting the Mother) Only your children. There were no other considerations, other influences?

MOTHER

Truly, one would say you are seeking to destroy my work. Well, Laura—leave!

VERA

Oh, yes, Mama!

POZNICHEV

(Smiling—in a low voice) No—she won't leave!

MOTHER

Oh, man! If I wasn't there to watch. Look, Poznichev—what was the origin of your terrible misunderstanding?

POZNICHEV

What, you don't know? I allowed myself to send an irritating person away.

MOTHER

Troukhasinsky?

POZNICHEV

Yes.

MOTHER

You had special reasons for being angry with him?

POZNICHEV

No.

MOTHER

He's antipathetic to you.

POZNICHEV

Not anymore!

MOTHER

Come on, you are reasonable—you are going to write him a letter—

POZNICHEV

Yes—

MOTHER

A nice letter.

POZNICHEV

To beg him to return. (To Laura) That's right, isn't it, Laura?

LAURA

But—

MOTHER

(Interrupting) Certainly!

POZNICHEV

I'll write. I'll write immediately. What do I want? The

happiness of my wife. If I annoy her I will be a wretch. Women are sensitive and the consequences so deplorable! I'll write. I'll write. (He sits at the back)

LAURA

It wasn't necessary to exasperate him. Look at him!

MOTHER

That's nothing. It's necessary to show him right off that the rules have been switched.

LAURA

Is it necessary to recall, Troukhasinsky? I'm afraid.

MOTHER

Of what?

LAURA

I'm afraid—That between these two men—

MOTHER

Don't be a child! All you must do is to be more cold to Troukhasinsky. He will understand—he will spare his visits. That will be better. That will be more prudent.

POZNICHEV

(Rising) Here—The letter—I knew quite well this would be Laura's first wish. I am happy to fulfill them. (He rings. Servant enters) I'll have it delivered, right? (A pause. He gives the letter to a Servant who leaves) You are joyful, Laura. Do you have any other desire? Look, Laura, don't be bothered. And you Vera—And you, charming Mama? There, frankly, without ceremony, sit down to eat. Share the cake—we are family. Here I am! Share!

MOTHER

I don't understand you. (To Vera) Come Vera, let's leave them alone. Once we are no longer here, you will reconcile very quickly.

VERA

(Reproachfully) Oh—Mama—Mama.

MOTHER

(With authority) Come! Come! (To Laura) Au revoir Laura! (She kisses her)

LAURA

You are going, you are leaving me alone.

POZNICHEV

Alone? I will be with you!

MOTHER

Your husband will remain with you. (Calling) Vera.

VERA

Au revoir, Laura—! Till later! (They leave)

POZNICHEV

They are leaving us alone like when we were engaged.

LAURA

Don't speak of those times.

POZNICHEV

(With a smile) Like before we were engaged, we were alone. Discreetly, your mother and your sister distanced themselves. You remember the room with the faded hangings in which I felt I loved you? You wore a hollowed-out corsage, hollowed out like your slip—It was by design we were left alone and that your throat was nude. I knew it. Still, I made the necessary gesture that you were expecting and that you are still expecting! (He leans over her)

LAURA

Let's still be sincere!

POZNICHEV

Are you forgetting, my little Laura, that certain situations can't be saved except by lies.

LAURA

I don't want anymore.

POZNICHEV

Bravo.

LAURA

I've hastened to shout the truth. I don't love you. I see plainly now, like that day I never loved you.

POZNICHEV

Me neither, me neither!

LAURA

If I am remaining with you, it's for my children's sake!

POZNICHEV

Precisely. Henceforth we are enemies that force has joined under the same roof—in the same room even.

LAURA

Oh! No! Not in one room. You are mistaken my friend. Not in one room. Don't count on that! You will never touch me again! Never! Never!

POZNICHEV

Consider! Henceforth my jealousy will be more clear-sighted. After a husband has spent the night in the arms of his wife, he's ready to believe whatever she wishes—until the next night. So that I may still be credulous, so that I may feel secure—If you value your life—don't repulse me—be prudent.

LAURA

No, I will not be prudent. You can kill me, but until my last breath, I will brave you.

POZNICHEV

Take care!

LAURA

You don't frighten me. From the moment that I remain

with you, you must understand that I am not one of those that recoil. I am resigned. I'm ready for everything on your part.

POZNICHEV

You don't want to hear reason—so be it—amuse yourself, my girl. The bridle's on your neck—Prance around—be crazy—I won't stop you. I will wait till you've exceeded certain limits and then—

LAURA

So much the worse. What must happen will happen!

POZNICHEV

I won't be merciful to you. Especially don't think that a lover, however strong and powerful he may be, will know how to protect you from my wrath. I say this to you. When the moment comes—you will see him flee before me. (A servant enters)

Servant

(Announcing) Mr. Troukhasinsky.

LAURA

Show him in. (The servant leaves)

POZNICHEV

(Ironic) I'm going away, I don't wish to disturb your effusions. He rushed, this brave musician. Only, I promise you that the day when it's a question of fleeing, he will be more prompt. You will see what a gallop, a musician is capable of! (He heads toward the door and stops) I don't wish to irritate you. (Leaves) I'm going.

TROUKHASINSKY

(Entering) Poor dear lady—

LAURA

Hello, my friend.

TROUKHASINSKY

How are you? You're not in pain. Reassure me.

LAURA

You see, I made an effort to get up. I'm a bit better.

TROUKHASINSKY

Thank God. Thank God.

LAURA

I am very grateful for your solicitude. You just received

a letter from my husband.

TROUKHASINSKY

(Feigning astonishment) A letter—from your husband—?

LAURA

They just delivered it to your home.

TROUKHASINSKY

I'll get it when I return. What's he want?

LAURA

You didn't know—and yet you came. You didn't recoil before his threats?

TROUKHASINSKY

I thought you were very ill—I had to see you.

LAURA

But, unfortunately, if you'd come an hour sooner, it would have been terrible, he would have hurled himself on you.

TROUKHASINSKY

And then?

LAURA

Then you've never seen his hands.

TROUKHASINSKY

His hands? And my cane? You've never seen it. Yes, my appearance is delicate—frail—a musician. But, it's unnecessary to be proud of it. I fence, I box, I swim. I have muscles of iron under an elegant envelope. A woman can lean on me.

LAURA

Yes, you are courageous!

TROUKHASINSKY

Just now I was at a club when a friend approached me and said "Poznichev's wife is very ill—she wanted—" I didn't hesitate for a second. I wanted to see you—imperatively.

LAURA

(Taking his hand) That's very sweet—more than sweet.

TROUKHASINSKY

And if he'd insulted me, I would have annihilated him in an act of cold rage. I cannot bear people of his sort. What do you want—my artistic nature has more affinity with the complacent husband than with the brute. I've got the weakness of being sensitive.

LAURA

You are chivalrous!

TROUKHASINSKY

It's my defect! If you knew how many boring things, bothers, even dangers, I owe to this weakness of soul. I've had duels—very serious ones—with pistols—with sabers.

LAURA

Really!

TROUKHASINSKY

If I were to consider—but I always follow my first action.

LAURA

That's the best.

TROUKHASINSKY

Not always—even now—

LAURA

Well?

TROUKHASINSKY

I regret coming.

LAURA

Oh.

TROUKHASINSKY

When I learned the thing—What had happened here—I had at first, only one idea—to fly to your assistance, because I thought you were in danger. I wanted to gently take your hands in mind and speak words that would console you. I thought I was in some way responsible.

LAURA

You weren't!

TROUKHASINSKY

As for me, I've experienced life so much, I was excessively moved by this misfortune—like a student. I pitied you.—Me, an egoist—Yes, you revealed to me the feeling of pity. I was outraged as if I'd seen the wrong they'd done you. You were unjustly struck. Unjustly—you deserved another destiny.

LAURA

(Discouraged) What do you want?

TROUKHASINSKY

(Sighing) Ah! How I regret having come. My visit will irritate your husband. He will become more violent, more cruel—He will torture you.

LAURA

No, I no longer fear him.

TROUKHASINSKY

(Astonished) Ah!

LAURA

(Looking him in the eyes) You are a man capable of defending a woman?

TROUKHASINSKY

(Troubled) I've proved it many times—most recently

still in Dresden.

LAURA

You aren't one of those who flee?

TROUKHASINSKY

I remain. (A silence)

LAURA

And yet (Changing her tone) you don't brutalize women, do you? Anyway no one can obtain anything from me except by gentleness—I ask only to obey!

TROUKHASINSKY

I am caressing.

LAURA

Is that really your nature? You mustn't deceive me.

TROUKHASINSKY

I am sincere.

LAURA

Then—Thanks for coming. I felt myself alone—My husband, you know him. My family—I can say it to you—My Mother loves me—but less than her ease. I cannot tell you how tired I was of existence; suddenly you came.

TROUKHASINSKY

(Fatuously) Ah!

LAURA

You came without having received his letter! You were kicked out of this house and bravely, you returned.

TROUKHASINSKY

(Modestly) It was quite natural.

LAURA

No—If you knew how much, after all that I've just seen, your attitude appears fine to me. Consoling. As for me, abandoned by the whole world, I don't know how to express my gratitude. I'll try—There (She kisses Troukhasinsky's hand—which he quickly withdraws)

TROUKHASINSKY

You are mad, Laura!

LAURA

(Violently) Why worry! He isn't here.

TROUKHASINSKY

Even if he were here. (Kissing her)

LAURA

(Leaning against Troukhasinsky) Tell me, you will protect me? You will defend me?

TROUKHASINSKY

You can be easy.

LAURA

I have confidence in you.

TROUKHASINSKY

You can do that!

LAURA

(Caressing his hair) You have long silky hair. I love your eyes—they're green like the depths of the sea.

TROUKHASINSKY

They're blue.

LAURA

I assure you they are deep green.

TROUKHASINSKY

Dear child, the greatest music critic in Berlin wrote they were blue.

LAURA

Never mind: there are clouds of blue waves in your eyes.

TROUKHASINSKY

Why are you shivering in my arms like a bird taken in a trap?

LAURA

I'm cold.

TROUKHASINSKY

You're feverish.

LAURA

I believe it.

TROUKHASINSKY

Go rest, my beloved.

LAURA

(Uneasy) No, no—

TROUKHASINSKY

For an hour.

LAURA

I'll obey you, but you'll wait for me—you won't go away.

TROUKHASINSKY

Yes, I'll wait for you.

LAURA

Then, escort me to the door. (She leans against him) I am heavy?

TROUKHASINSKY

No.

LAURA

Then carry me—

TROUKHASINSKY

No—craziness—(Laura leaves. Troukhasinsky rings. A servant enters) It was you who recently delivered a letter to me on behalf of your master?

SERVANT

It was I, sir.

TROUKHASINSKY

Listen (Giving him money) If Madame asks you to whom you delivered the letter, you will say you left it with the concierge because I was out; that you didn't see me.

SERVANT

I will lie, sir.

TROUKHASINSKY

Yes—you will. You understand?

SERVANT

Perfectly, sir. The gentleman has other orders to give me?

TROUKHASINSKY

No—give me a light for my cigarette, a cushion for my back, and a stool for my feet.

POZNICHEV

(Entering) Hello.

CURTAIN

ACT FOUR

DOCTOR

Well, my dear friends, goodbye.

LAURA

Already.

DOCTOR

It's two o'clock in the morning, I've got to be at the hospital at eight o'clock.

TROUKHASINSKY

Stay still, I am going in a half hour. I'd like to play my sonata for two hands one more time. Would you like to, Madame!

LAURA

What do you think?

DOCTOR

It's fine, you know.

LAURA

It's very fine.

DOCTOR

Yes, it does produce a certain effect on your guests.

LAURA

There's a passage in which, I'm a little uncomfortable. You'll excuse me?

TROUKHASINSKY

Oh! Besides it's the part we're going to repeat right now.

DOCTOR

Ah, yes, you will play it together in two weeks at a concert at the English club. Your husband will be back.

LAURA

I hope so. But he's almost always in the country.

TROUKHASINSKY

He doesn't like Petersburg anymore.

LAURA

He's with his farmers. At the moment he's near Astrakhan.

TROUKHASINSKY

2,000 kilometers from Petersburg.

DOCTOR

You astonish me. He's not so far off. I received a letter from one of my friends who lives in Kursk. He was there three days ago.

TROUKHASINSKY

What?

LAURA

He returned to Astrakhan then because I received a telegram from him this afternoon. That's bizarre.

TROUKHASINSKY

A telegram you were expecting? A response?

LAURA

No—a banal telegram.

DOCTOR

Perhaps he has an adventure in Kursk, your brave agriculturist—he intends to make you think he's in Astrakhan.

TROUKHASINSKY

That will be funny.

LAURA

It's likely.

DOCTOR

Excuse this supposition in bad taste, Madame, and *au revoir*.

LAURA

Au revoir! You will indeed be looking yourself for your overcoat. The last guest left an hour ago and I didn't want to oblige the servants to remain awake any later.

DOCTOR

You are too humane. I won't awaken anyone. I will

myself lean on the electric button in the antechamber to the right; I will very quietly shut the street door. (He leaves)

LAURA

My darling! Ah, soon we will no longer have any more such nights. He's going to come back.

TROUKHASINSKY

We'll have the days. Do you really think he was at Kursk?

LAURA

Who knows?

TROUKHASINSKY

Why in that case, he may arrive soon?

LAURA

Bah! Since he's not here today.

TROUKHASINSKY

What time does the last train arrive?

LAURA

At eleven.

TROUKHASINSKY

Yes—

LAURA

And then, if he wasn't at Kursk, I have his dispatch.

TROUKHASINSKY

Kiss me. You must be exhausted, my darling—Do you want me to leave you?

LAURA

Oh! This is the last night that he's leaving us, perhaps—Come.

TROUKHASINSKY

Wait.

LAURA

What?

TROUKHASINSKY

We must put the lights out since the servants are asleep.

LAURA

You're right. I'm going to put them out. Go—and don't make any noise going through the small salon.

TROUKHASINSKY

Bah! You'd think Ivanoff was there. We can talk and even resume my sonata.

LAURA

Oh! Now!

TROUKHASINSKY

Only the Andante La, Co, la, la, la, la!

LAURA

Yes, yes—whatever you like.

TROUKHASINSKY

You're sweet.

LAURA

You love me.

TROUKHASINSKY

Put out the lights.

LAURA

Who's there?

POZNICHEV

(Entering) Why, it's me.

LAURA

Ah! You frightened me! I didn't hear you come.

POZNICHEV

I didn't want to wake anyone.

LAURA

Your luggage?

POZNICHEV

The porter hadn't gone to bed yet, I sent him to the train station.

LAURA

But why did you return so abruptly? It's not a misfortune which brings you?

POZNICHEV

No, no—I don't think so.

LAURA

And how were you able to telephone me from Astrakhan this afternoon?

POZNICHEV

My steward had orders; it was he who sent you this dispatch.

LAURA

You intended to surprise me?

POZNICHEV

Indeed, I have the air of a jealous husband.

LAURA

You're not ashamed of it?

POZNICHEV

You had guests tonight?

LAURA

The porter told you—

POZNICHEV

I don't question my help. No! But it stinks of tobacco.

LAURA

Indeed, I had a few people for dinner—My Mother, Doctor Ivanoff—

POZNICHEV

Troukhasinsky, also, I believe—That must be charming. I would really have liked to arrive a bit sooner. Still, it's lacking! Ah, why no. Music. Come my dear friend! You weren't waiting for me?

TROUKHASINSKY

I remained to look over a passage in a sonata with Madame.

POZNICHEV

Yes—yes.

LAURA

It wasn't easy to decipher.

TROUKHASINSKY

No, not easy, not easy at all.

POZNICHEV

And then the time was ill chosen.

TROUKHASINSKY-

What do you mean!

POZNICHEV

Two in the morning. That's not the time to make music. The most brilliant virtuoso no longer has abilities, right, my dear friend?

TROUKHASINSKY

There's no hour for the brave.

POZNICHEV

For the brave—Evidently.

LAURA

You'll allow us to resume?

TROUKHASINSKY

Oh, dear Madame, it's very late indeed. Your husband is tired. I don't wish to be importunate. No, that would be indiscreet. Tomorrow at five.

POZNICHEV

Right. Tomorrow you will do what you wish.

TROUKHASINSKY

Madame—dear friend—Ah!

LAURA

What is it?

TROUKHASINSKY

Your husband shook my hand very hard.

POZNICHEV

Pardon. I have rough paws.

TROUKHASINSKY

No—but the stone of one of my rings hurt me.

POZNICHEV

You wear too many rings!

LAURA

Excuse my husband; he lives with simple folk.

POZNICHEV

Folk of a primitive simplicity, dear friend. By the way, you know the son of the tavern keeper killed his wife.

LAURA

No—That beautiful girl.

POZNICHEV

Too beautiful. She was cheating on him.

TROUKHASINSKY

Was it a certainty?

POZNICHEV

A certainty. He didn't see them—what one calls seeing—But if one doesn't kill after having seen—

TROUKHASINSKY

He must be overwhelmed with remorse.

POZNICHEV

No. I talked with him. He was calm. He'd found peace.

TROUKHASINSKY

He's a brute, your peasant.

POZNICHEV

No! No! He's a lad who did precisely what he ought to have done—what must be done.

TROUKHASINSKY

You know quite well, my dear friend, you make me tremble.

POZNICHEV

I see that plainly.

TROUKHASINSKY

Oh! I said that to laugh.

POZNICHEV

Let's laugh! You're not well?

LAURA

I have a headache. I'm going to call my chambermaid.

POZNICHEV

Don't bother that girl at two in the morning. Am I not near you to care for you? A glass of sugar—water and orange flower, right? There's a flask in your room. I'm going to find it. (Poznichev leaves)

LAURA

You won't leave me alone with him. I'm afraid.

TROUKHASINSKY

You're crazy! He's full of concern for you; he's uneasy over your health. He is caring for you.

LAURA

He grasped that pretext to get into my room to see if the bed is in disorder. I know him! He wouldn't recoil before an assassination, I am sure of it. You mustn't abandon me. Let's leave, I beg you.

TROUKHASINSKY

You are going to escape into the street in a low-cut dress?

LAURA

Well, let's scream out the truth to him.

TROUKHASINSKY

You are senseless! He will kill us.

LAURA

We will defend ourselves. Doubtless he's armed. And you, my darling?

TROUKHASINSKY

My revolver is in my overcoat.

LAURA

Down below in the antechamber. Go down quickly. Go find it.

TROUKHASINSKY

I hear him coming back.

LAURA

I am lost.

TROUKHASINSKY

No! No! I will make a pretense of leaving, I won't leave the house I'll come back to defend you.

LAURA

You promise me, you swear to me?

TROUKHASINSKY

What a child! (Poznichev reenters)

POZNICHEV

Here, drink.

LAURA

Thanks.

POZNICHEV

Are you better?

LAURA

Yes.

POZNICHEV

Well, *au revoir*, dear friend. You see, Laura is ill. I am tired. Till tomorrow.

TROUKHASINSKY

Soon, Madame.

LAURA

Soon, dear sir—

POZNICHEV

I won't accompany you. You'll excuse me.

TROUKHASINSKY

Stay, stay. (Exit Troukhasinsky)

POZNICHEV

What a charming friend, right?

LAURA

Huh? I beg your pardon. I didn't hear.

POZNICHEV

I said: What a charming friend.

LAURA

Yes!

POZNICHEV

There's no one below to help him dress. That's not nice. I am going to go down.

LAURA

No, indeed. He understands very well that you are tired.

POZNICHEV

Don't you think it's funny, Laura?

LAURA

What?

POZNICHEV

It's funny. All the servants went to bed and yet there's still one guest in the house. That's funny.

LAURA

No—We must have been making music a bit late.

POZNICHEV

I know. I know. But still the valet ought to have been waiting. I'm not addressing any reproach to you, my darling, but it's not good to send the servants to their rooms with a friend still in the house: You might need services! It's annoying! It's annoying!

LAURA

You attach such importance.

POZNICHEV

No, no—I don't say it serious. I said it's annoying it's very annoying. I tell you, servants don't have delicate feelings. They won't believe you had pity on their exhaustion when you sent them to bed, little imprudent one!

LAURA

Ah!

POZNICHEV

What?

LAURA

It's that uproar, I wasn't expecting it.

POZNICHEV

Why it's nothing; it's our friend who left.

LAURA

I was surprised—I wasn't expecting it.

POZNICHEV

How easily you upset yourself, my darling—it's a disquieting sensitivity.

LAURA

Yes, I don't feel very well. Good night, my friend.

POZNICHEV

A moment longer!

LAURA

But—

POZNICHEV

One moment. I haven't seen you for two weeks. I am happy for a *tête-à-tête*, because he left us in a *tête-à-tête*.

LAURA

That's quite natural.

POZNICHEV

It's very natural. I foresaw it, you remember—? I told you that he would flee and that you would remain with me.

LAURA

I don't understand.

POZNICHEV

Didn't you hear as the door slammed? He left quickly, as if he was fleeing and he slammed the door violently. He must be running in the street. He must be far away if he's still running.

LAURA

But, yet, Poznichev—

POZNICHEV

Well.

LAURA

You seem to think.

POZNICHEV

I don't seem, I don't think—I know.

LAURA

That's not true! That's an infamy! That man is only a friend for me.

POZNICHEV

That's possible. Everything is possible.

LAURA

Indeed you feel I am speaking the truth!

POZNICHEV

No.

LAURA

Would you like me to swear on the head of my mother?

POZNICHEV

I don't see any inconvenience.

LAURA

On the head of my children.

POZNICHEV

That, no.

LAURA

Still, you know I love them? I would willingly die for them.

POZNICHEV

It's enough to die on one's own account.

LAURA

Poznichev! Poznichev!

POZNICHEV

Well you shut up, you're mad!

LAURA

I beg you! I beg you!

POZNICHEV

Come on! Shut up! You mustn't awaken the children! Is it permitted to shout like that in the presence of a revolver? I remembered I had this weapon in my pocket. I am putting it in without a holster in its bag. It's not prudent to carry a weapon. You lean on the trigger without intending. Detonation! Mustn't awaken the children!

LAURA

This is infamous. You don't have the right to torture me like this.

POZNICHEV

Me—torture you? Take care. You no longer have your cool, you no longer have your good sense.

LAURA

Yes, yes—This is monstrous! You are a wretch!

POZNICHEV

Take care! Take care! You're going to betray yourself. You're going to confess.

LAURA

I have nothing to confess. You are aware of everything

in my life.

POZNICHEV

Speak! Speak!

LAURA

You are only a coward!

POZNICHEV

A coward. Ah! Ah! You think you are talking to someone else.

LAURA

You are all cowards! No! No! Not all! Someone's coming! Someone's coming!

POZNICHEV

Enter. (Enter Gregor)

GREGOR

Pardon, sir, these are the bags. They are below. But as I saw the light here, I thought perhaps you would expect them. Should I bring them up?

POZNICHEV

No—Go to bed, my friend!

GREGOR

Good night, sir, good night, Madame.

LAURA

Gregor!

GREGOR

Madame has an order to give me?

LAURA

Yes. If your wife is up, let her be so obliging as to come help me undress—my chambermaid's asleep.

GREGOR

It's that my wife is in bed. She went to bed after Mr. Troukhasinsky left—but I am going tell her to come up.

LAURA

No, no—It's unnecessary—only call my chambermaid.

POZNICHEV

Why, my dear friend, what need have we of Gregor? We will ring for her.

LAURA

Well—ring!

GREGOR

Good night, sir.

LAURA

You rang?

POZNICHEV

No.

LAURA

I intend for someone to come! I will call! I will call!

POZNICHEV

Will you shut up?

LAURA

You don't have the right! You don't have the right!

POZNICHEV

I don't have the right to talk with my wife after returning from a trip?

LAURA

You know perfectly well what I mean.

POZNICHEV

No, explain!

LAURA

I'll defend myself!

POZNICHEV

Against who? Against me? Ah, my poor girl.

LAURA

Then you don't intend to do me harm. Answer me!

POZNICHEV

You don't want to die, huh? You cling to life?

LAURA

Yes.

POZNICHEV

You've always clung to it.

LAURA

Yes.

POZNICHEV

You never seriously thought of disappearing? Really you can admit it to me?

LAURA

Yes, yes, I was so unhappy.

POZNICHEV

Then today you are no longer so unhappy?

LAURA

No!

POZNICHEV

You are happy.

LAURA

That's saying too much.

POZNICHEV

Still, you have a little happiness. I'm not the one who is giving it to you. But you have a little happiness.

LAURA

Poznichev, why are you so proud? Why have you remained so far away from me?

POZNICHEV

That's admirable—wasn't it you who insisted on it?

LAURA

You didn't have to obey me. You ought to have persuaded me—to get me back.

POZNICHEV

Speak, speak! I've never seen you like this.

LAURA

You know me badly, you don't know me. I am no longer the little girl I used to be.

POZNICHEV

I've suspected that.

LAURA

I am a woman.

POZNICHEV

Love has transformed you—Let's render thanks to love.

LAURA

No, Poznichev, it's very natural. I've got the age of happiness.

POZNICHEV

Congratulations.

LAURA

If you want—if you want.

POZNICHEV

Curious! Very curious. Why weren't you this way two weeks ago? You hadn't reached the age of happiness, right? You needed two weeks.

LAURA

I didn't dare to confess it to you. We don't talk to each other.

POZNICHEV

Yes. It requires exceptional circumstances for you to confess to me your secret fondness. I have to surprise you at night with your lover.

LAURA

No! No!

POZNICHEV

You must be afraid.

LAURA

You are mistaken.

POZNICHEV

Of vice, then?

LAURA

Perhaps—

POZNICHEV

Ah! Ah!

LAURA

Poznichev!

POZNICHEV

Then—tonight—you love me.

LAURA

I'm begging you.

POZNICHEV

You know very well that, now, I will love you perhaps to madness. I will be enslaved by you again.

LAURA

That will be fine!

POZNICHEV

Yes! Yes!

LAURA

My darling! My darling!

POZNICHEV

Well, come kiss me. Come! Come—Are you afraid?

LAURA

Afraid? Oh, no!

POZNICHEV

How pale you are! It's the emotion of love. Come on, my little one.

LAURA

You love me, don't you? You love me.

POZNICHEV

Come into my arms. (He strangles her) Whew!

CURTAIN

ABOUT THE AUTHOR

Frank J. Morlock has written and translated many plays since retiring from the legal profession in 1992. His translations have also appeared on Project Gutenberg, the Alexandre Dumas Père web page, Literature in the Age of Napoléon, Infinite Artistries.com, and Munsey's (formerly Blackmask). In 2006 he received an award from the North American Jules Verne Society for his translations of Verne's plays. He lives and works in México.

www.ingramcontent.com/pod-product-compliance
Lightning Source LLC
LaVergne TN
LVHW041617070426
835507LV00008B/293